Quick-and-Easy Learning Games
Phonics

by Wiley Blevins

SCHOLASTIC
PROFESSIONAL BOOKS

New York • Toronto • London • Auckland • Sydney

Dedication

I would like to dedicate this book to my former students, whose zest for learning, innocence, and endless laughter have given me so much personal and professional satisfaction. I would also like to dedicate this book to my grandmother, who never had the opportunity to learn to read. It is because of her that I became a teacher.

Acknowledgments

I would like to thank Jeanne Chall, Marilyn Jager Adams, M.E. Curtis, and the many other professors, colleagues, and classroom teachers who have taught me so much about how children learn to read.

Editor: Joan Novelli
Cover design by Jaime Lucero and Vincent Ceci
Cover and interior illustration by Paige Billin-Frye
Interior design by Sydney Wright

ISBN 0-590-96380-5

Contents

The Role of Phonics in a Balanced Reading Program

Recently, because of declines in reading test scores and concerns about the lack of skills instruction in schools, there has been a renewed interest in phonics instruction. I believe that the teaching of phonics in a meaningful context is an important element in a balanced reading program—one that addresses the developmental needs of children based on the stage of reading they are at.

To understand how best to meet the needs of beginning readers, here is an overview of the early stages of reading development. During these stages, children learn sound/spelling correspondences and the principles of blending. According to Juel (1991), these stages include:

1. Selective-cue stage: During this stage, readers pay more attention to contextual cues, such as context and picture clues. Stories that contain repetitive text structures or rhyming patterns are common reading during this stage and help children to predict words while reading.

2. Spelling-sound stage: During this stage, readers focus on graphophonic cues. It is during this stage that phonics instruction plays a crucial role as children are attending to each letter in words.

3. Automatic stage: During this stage, readers utilize both contextual (meaning) and graphophonic (phonics) cues. It is during this stage that readers develop fluency.

When I think about these stages, I ask myself, What do children need instructionally to effectively progress through each?

Reading programs that focus only on the selective-cue stage are referred to as meaning-oriented programs. Although most of these programs do contain some phonics instruction, there are few opportunities for children to practice their phonics skills with connected text. Therefore, children tend to undervalue the utility of the phonics skills they are learning. Connected texts should contain a large portion of words that can be decoded based on the sounds children have been taught up to that point. Although most practice stories in these programs do contain words that begin with a target sound taught, the words aren't decodable based on the sounds children have been previously taught. Therefore, these children are forced to rely on meaning cues, losing out on important blending practice.

Programs that focus only on phonics are referred to as phonics-oriented programs. Phonics instruction void of a print-rich environment with multiple language experiences can be dull and can leave children unaware that reading is more than just sounding out words, it is also making meaning from text.

A balanced approach to reading instruction emphasizes both contextual (meaning) and graphophonic (phonics) cues, and provides reading support materials so children have multiple opportunities to practice these cueing systems. Phonics is only one important element of this reading instruction. In the context of great literature and varied language experiences, children can and will learn to read with the aid of a strong phonics program, attention to prerequisite skills such as phonemic awareness and alphabet recognition, and the skill of a caring teacher. Teaching children to read and instilling in them a love for reading is one of the best gifts any teacher can give.

Much success,

Wiley Blevins

 # About this Book

The best way for children to apply their phonics skills is through reading simple, engaging stories that contain a large portion of words that can be blended based on the sounds learned. In addition to the reading of easy text, learning games are an enjoyable way for children to practice and reinforce their phonics skills. Games are especially useful as learning tools for children who have had difficulty with more traditional learning approaches.

Quick-and-Easy Learning Games: Phonics focuses on children's knowledge of sound/spelling correspondences and their ability to blend words. Some of the benefits of integrating these games into your reading program follow.

- Phonics games provide children with a way to assess their own phonics abilities through the immediate feedback they receive while playing.

- Watching children play phonics games serves as a valuable assessment tool for you, letting you pick up on strengths and areas of need as children interact in a relaxed atmosphere.

- On a social level, game playing can help children learn to work cooperatively, give and take praise and criticism, teach others, and accept successes and failures.

The games in *Quick-and-Easy Learning Games: Phonics* have been sequenced, using a scope and sequence followed by many early reading programs. However, most of the games can be adapted to review phonics skills other than those designated.

Preparing to Play

Each of the 13 games includes the game boards and cards your students need to play, plus spinners and dice as necessary. To support your instructional goals, each game also comes with a page of teaching materials that includes:

- Players: the recommended number of players in each game group
- Skill: the phonics focus in the particular game
- To Play: step-by-step directions to share with students
- Variations: suggestions for making the game easier, more challenging, and so on

Most of the games in the book can be put together in well under an hour; in fact, some can be duplicated and made ready for play in minutes. The following suggestions will help you adapt the games for your class:

1. Enlarge game boards, game cards, and other game pieces on a photocopier, if desired.

2. Paste game boards onto larger pieces of colored construction paper before decorating and laminating. (When game boards are on two pages, tape the halves together.)

3. Transfer word and word building cards onto index cards, then laminate.

4. Paste picture cards onto index cards and laminate.

5. Place the games in an accessible area of your classroom and encourage children to play during free time.

One of the best ways to teach children how to play the games—and maximize their gains—is to model as you plan to use them. This can be achieved by playing for both players, playing against children while assisting them, or teaching one group of children how to play the game and then having them demonstrate it for their classmates.

Getting Families Involved

You might find it helpful to make extra games so that children can take them home to play with family members. Getting families involved in their children's growing literacy development will have tremendous payoffs.

Professional Resources

Adams, Marilyn Jager. (1990) *Beginning to Read: Thinking and Learning About Print.* Cambridge: Massachusetts Institute of Technology.

Anderson, R.C., Hiebert, E.H., Scott, J.A., and Wilkinson, I.A.G. (1985) *Becoming a Nation of Readers: The Report of the Commission on Reading.* Champaign, IL: Center for the Study of Reading.

Baltis, Joyce, Schafer, Susan. (1996) *School Guide to Balanced Reading K–2*. New York: Scholastic Professional Books.

Chall, Jeanne. (1983) *Stages of Reading Development*. New York: McGraw-Hill.

Honig, Bill. (1995) *How Should We Teach Our Children to Read?* Center for Systemic School Reform. San Francisco State University.

Juel, Connie. (1991) "Beginning Reading." In R. Barr, M. Kamil, P. Mosenthal, and P.D. Pearson, eds. *Handbook of Reading Research*, Volume II (pp. 759-788). New York: Longman.

Wagstaff, Janiel. (1994) *Phonics that Work: New Strategies for the Reading/Writing Classroom*. New York: Scholastic Professional Books.

Go to School

Skill: consonants

MATERIALS

game board (see pages 10–11)

place marker for each player

die (see page 12)

SETUP

▲ Make a copy of the game board and die. Construct the die by folding along the dotted lines and using tape to attach the die tabs to the die squares.

TO PLAY

1 Each player chooses a place marker and puts it on START (the school bus).

2 The first player throws the die and moves his or her marker along the game board path the number of spaces on the die. (The object of the game is to drive the school bus to the school.)

3 The player then states the name of the consonant on the game board space and says a word that begins with the sound the consonant stands for. For example, if the player lands on a space with the consonant *t*, he or she might say "t . . . table." If the player is unable to state the consonant's name or a word that begins with that consonant sound, he or she skips a turn.

4 Each player continues in turn. The first player to reach FINISH (the school) wins.

Variations

• **Make It More Challenging:** Have more skilled players write the words they state on a sheet of paper.

• **Final Consonant Sounds:** In this game, each player states a word that ends with the sound the consonant stands for. Prepare the game board by replacing the letters *h* and *qu* with *x*. Write the new letters on self-stick tags or small pieces of white tape.

• **Digraphs and Blends:** Replace consonants on the game board with digraphs (*ch, th, sh, wh, ph*) and blends (*bl, br, cl, cr, dr, fl, fr, gl, gr, pl, pr, sc, sk, sl, sm, sn, sp, st, sw, tr, tw*).

• **Vowels:** Replace consonants on the game board with short vowels (*a, e, i, o, u*), long vowel spellings (*ai, ay, ea, ee, ie, y, igh, oa, ow*), diphthongs and variant vowels (*oi, oy, au, aw, ou, ow, oo*), or *r*-controlled vowels (*ar, er, ir, or, ur*).

Go to School
Game Board

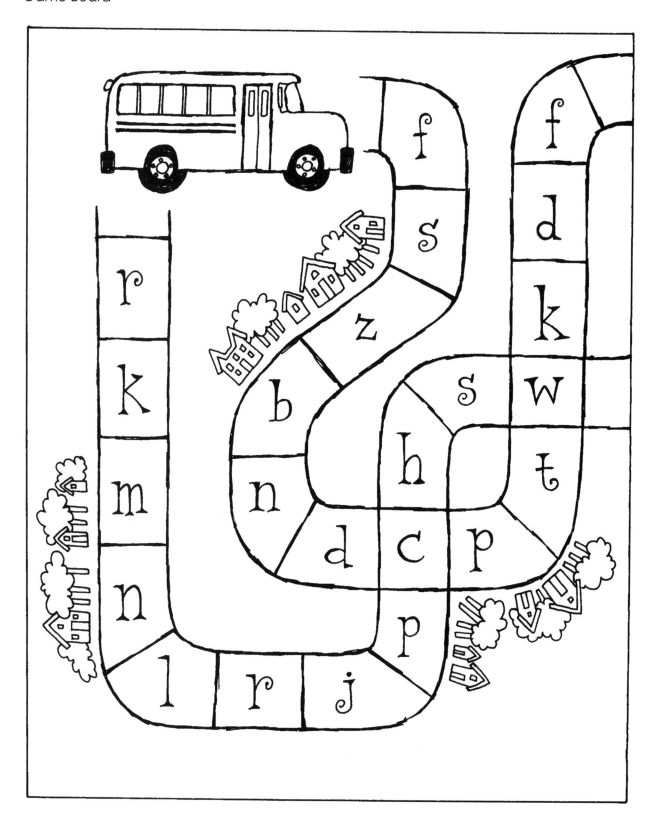

Go to School
Game Board

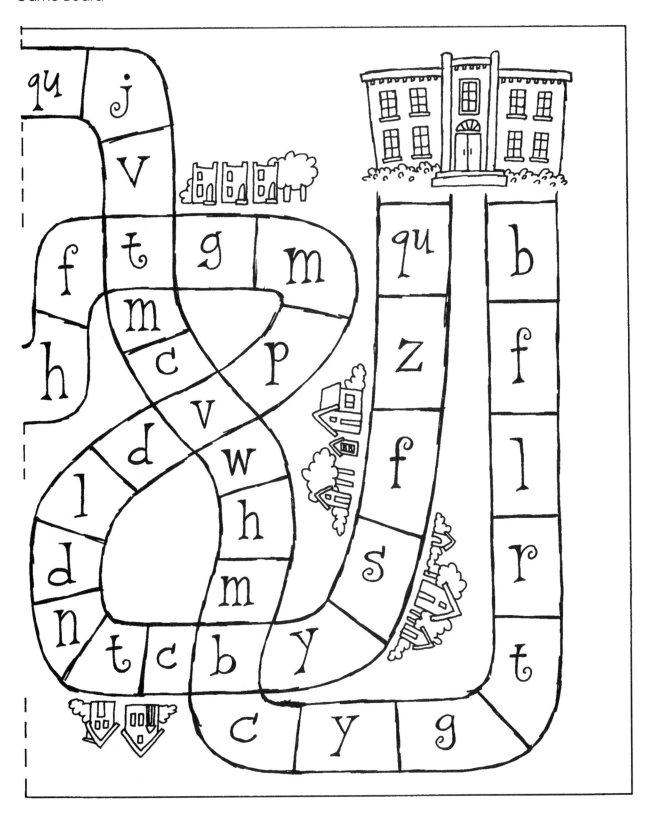

 # Go to School
Number Die

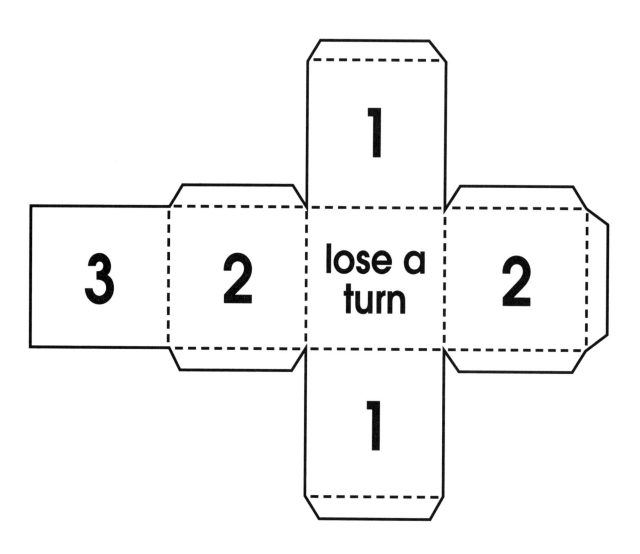

Spin It!

Skill: short vowels

MATERIALS

3 spinners (see pages 14–15)

paper and pencils

SETUP

▲ Copy and cut out the three spinners and dials. Paste them in sequence on a piece of tag board or the inside of a folder.

▲ Using a brass fastener, attach the dials to the spinners. (You might also want to make these from tag board.)

TO PLAY

1 Each player in turn spins all three spinners. The player writes the letters selected by the spinner dials in order—Spinner 1, first; Spinner 2, second; Spinner 3, third.

2 If a word can be formed from these letters, the player states the word aloud and writes it on his or her paper. Each word earns one point. Proper names, such as *Sam* or *Pat*, are allowed.

3 The first player to get 10 points wins.

Variations

• Change the Rules: Let children place their letters in any order to form words.

• Make New Spinners: Occasionally replace the spinners to update the game. (Use the blank spinner.) Suggestions follow:

Spinner 1: Replace the consonants with digraphs and blends.

Spinner 2: Replace the short vowels with long vowel digraphs (*ai, ay, ea, ee, ie, igh, y, oa, ow*).

Spinner 3: Replace some of the ending consonants with *ck, ff, ll, ss, ch, sh,* and *th.*

Spin It!
Spinners

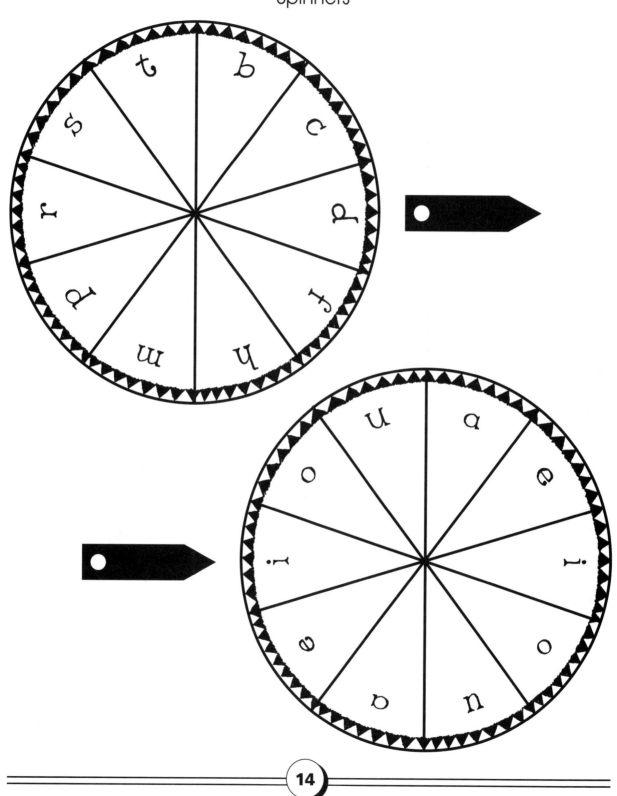

Spin It!
Spinners

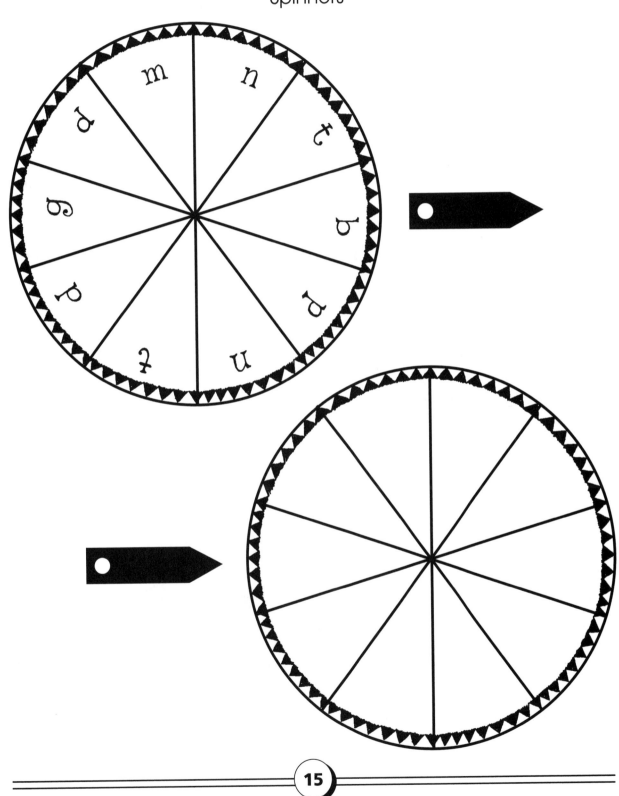

Frog Hop

Skill: short vowels

MATERIALS

game board (see pages 17–18)
game cards (see pages 19–20)
place marker for each player

SETUP

▲ Make a copy of the game board and game cards. On the back of each game card, write the answer or completed word.

▲ Shuffle the cards and place them faceup on the game board.

TO PLAY

1 Each player chooses a place marker and puts it on START.

2 The first player picks a card and moves his or her marker along the game board path to the next space with the short vowel that completes the word on the card. For example, if the player picks a card with *p__g*, he or she must move to the next *i* space. (Decide together what happens if a child chooses an incorrect short vowel.) Players can use the picture on each card as a clue.

3 Each player continues in turn. The first player to reach FINISH wins.

Variations

• Long Vowels: Make picture cards of objects that contain multiple spellings of the long vowels (ai, ay, ea, ee, ie, igh, y, oa, ow). The pictures might show *train, rain, mail, nail, hay, play, crayon, bean, leaf, peach, peanut, sea, deer, sleep, street, feet, wheel, teeth,* *fifteen, bee, knee, three, pie, tie, fly, sky, cry, boat, coat, soap, road, toast, goat, loaf, toad, snow, bowl, arrow, window.* Using small, self-stick tags, replace the short vowels on the game board with the long vowel spellings. Play the game as before.

Frog Hop
Game Board

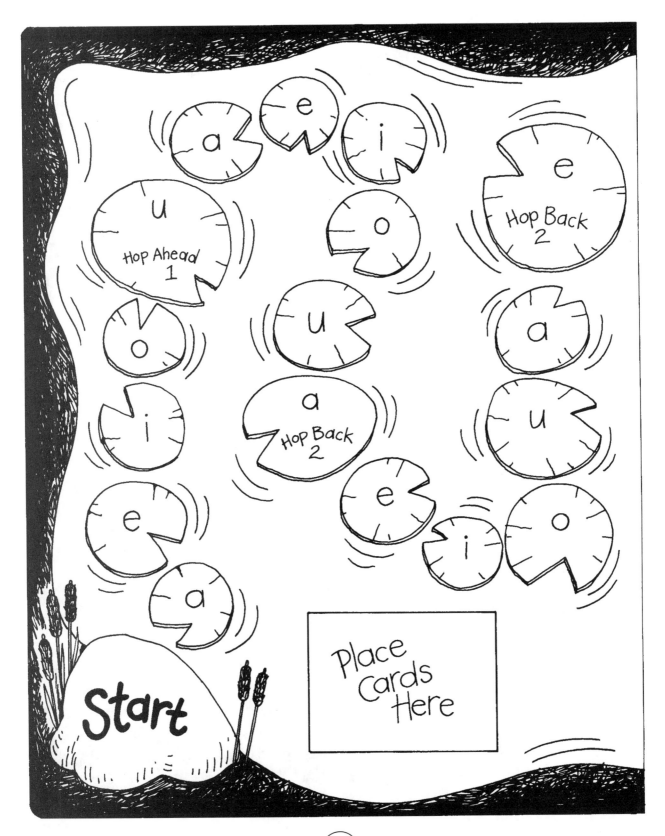

Frog Hop
Game Board

Frog Hop
Game Cards

c _ t	b _ g	
h _ t	f _ n	h _ nd
v _ n	t _ n	h _ n
j _ t	w _ b	n _ st
d _ sk	p _ g	h _ ll

Frog Hop
Game Cards

l _ ps	g _ ft	
k _ ck	s _ x	fr _ g
s _ ck	m _ p	b _ x
d _ g	r _ g	b _ g
n _ t	s _ n	c _ p

Build a House

Skill: phonograms

MATERIALS

game boards (see pages 22–23)
game cards (see pages 24-25)
space markers/tokens

SETUP

▲ Make a copy of the game boards and game cards. Game cards are provided for two to four games.

▲ Place the game cards facedown on the game board.

TO PLAY

1 Each player or team chooses a house to build, then draws a card from the card pile.

2 If a word can be formed by combining the consonant or blend on the card and one of the phonograms on the house, the player covers that square on the house with a marker. The player then returns the card to the bottom of the pile. If a word cannot be formed, the player just returns the card to the bottom of the pile and waits until the next turn.

3 Each player or team continues in turn. The first player to build a house (fill all the spaces in his or her house) wins.

Variations

• To Vary the Difficulty: Mix and match the game boards and game pieces to the level of difficulty desired. For example, to simplify the game, use only three phonograms. Write each phonogram three times on the house in random order. This allows players to focus on word families. (Players may not form the same word twice.)

• Make New Games: Using other phonograms, make new houses. You might choose to use phonograms from your weekly spelling list.

Build a House
Game Board

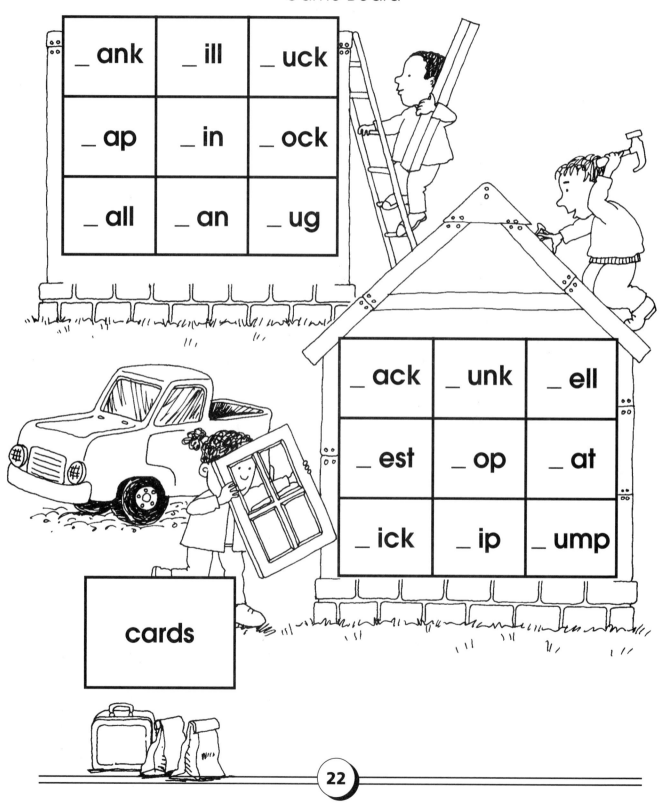

_ ank	_ ill	_ uck
_ ap	_ in	_ ock
_ all	_ an	_ ug

_ ack	_ unk	_ ell
_ est	_ op	_ at
_ ick	_ ip	_ ump

cards

Build a House
Game Board

_ ash	_ ine	_ ake
_ ice	_ ore	_ ate
_ ink	_ ame	_ ight

_ eat	_ ide	_ oke
_ ain	_ ing	_ ale
_ aw	_ ay	_ or

cards

Build a House
Game Cards

b	c	d	f
g	h	j	k
l	m	n	p
qu	r	s	t
v	w	y	z
free space	b	r	lose a turn

Build a House
Game Cards

bl	**br**	**cl**	**cr**
dr	**fl**	**fr**	**gr**
pl	**pr**	**gl**	**tr**
st	**sn**	**sm**	**sp**
sl	**sw**	**ch**	**sh**
free space	**th**	**wh**	lose a turn

Vowel Checkers

Skill: final e

MATERIALS

game board (see page 27)

24 checkers or markers (12 of one color, 12 of another color)

SETUP

▲ Make a copy of the game board. Set up the game as you would a regular checkers game. You can also use a ready-made checkerboard and checkers. If so, use self-stick tags and write the words provided on page 27 on the checkerboard.

·········· **TO PLAY** ··········

1 The game is played just like checkers, except players must read the word on each space he or she lands on. If a player cannot read the word, he or she returns to the original space. You might wish to review with players the following rules for playing checkers:

• Players take turns, moving one checker per turn. The checkers may be moved diagonally forward one square. For example, the player using the shaded squares can move his or her checkers on shaded squares only.

• A player can capture an opponent's checker by jumping over it. The square behind the checker being jumped must be empty. The player then takes the jumped checker and places it to the side of the game board. Players must jump other checkers when they can. A player can jump more than one checker at a time, provided the moves are forward.

Variations

• Short Vowels: Replace the words on the checkerboard with short vowel words.

• Multiple Spellings of Long Vowels: Replace the words on the checkerboard with words containing the multiple spellings of each long vowel (*a_e, ai, ay, e_e, e, ea, ee, i_e, ie, igh, y, o_e, oa, ow, u_e*).

Vowel Checkers
Game Board

grade	made	pet	Pete	pin	pine	rod	rode
Sam	same	at	ate	grad	grade	past	paste
rip	ripe	cub	cube	mat	mate	can	cane
plan	plane	bit	bite	hug	huge	not	note
fat	fate	hid	hide	kit	kite	Jan	Jane
us	use	hat	hate	rid	ride	quit	quite
glob	globe	hop	hope	cap	cape	Tim	time
fin	fine	rob	robe	man	mane	tap	tape

Sound Bingo

Skill: long vowels

MATERIALS

game board (see page 29)

space markers

SETUP

▲ Make copies of the game board. Use the words here to fill in the cards. Put the words in a different order for each card. Also, write each word on a small slip of paper and place in a bag.

Game 1 (Long A and Long E): *make, bake, pail, snail, rain, chain, train, wait, day, say, play, stay, bee, tree, seed, speed, week, queen, keep, sheep, street, leaf, bean, team*

Game 2 (Long I, Long O, and Long U): *pie, tie, fly, cry, spy, sigh, high, bike, lime, kite, boat, load, soap, coach, snow, grow, flow, toe, goes, bone, hope, home, cute, huge*

TO PLAY

1 Sound Bingo is played just like regular bingo. Before the game begins, give each player a game board and ample space markers. The caller draws one slip of paper from the bag and reads the word aloud.

2 If a player's game board contains that word, he or she places a marker over the space.

3 The first player to get five markers in a row either vertically, horizontally, or diagonally, yells "Sound Bingo." The player then reads the words aloud in the row as the caller checks them against the slips of paper drawn from the bag. If these match, the player wins.

4 Players then clear their boards, the slips of paper go back in the bag, and a new game begins.

Variations

• More Long Vowels: Use other words with long vowel spellings.

• Blends: Use your own word lists or the following list for making game boards containing blends: *black, brown, clean, crop, drop, flat, free, glow, green, plan, present, stamp, small, snake, speak, tree, sleep, scare, swing, twin, splash, spring, square, string.*

Sound Bingo

Game Board

SOUND BINGO

		FREE		

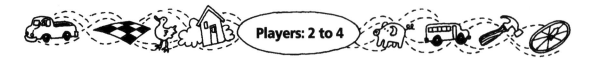

Raceway

Skill: long vowels

MATERIALS

game board (see pages 31–32)
die (see page 12)
place marker for each player

SETUP

▲ Make a copy of the game board and die. Construct the die by folding along the dotted lines and using tape to attach the die tabs to the die squares.

▲ Make an answer key card for players to check if they are challenged during the game. Include the following words: *rain, plea, play, bean, keep, snow, seep, soap, mean, moan, toast, reed, read, road, raid, monkey, tea, tow, toe, tie, fleas, flies, flows, train, honey, eat, oat, deep, fleet, float, seal, sail, key, goes, sea, see, say, sow, grow, gray, beat, beet, boat, bait, pea, pay, pie, tree, tray, beach, clean, wait, leaf.*

TO PLAY

1 Each player chooses a place marker and puts it on START (the beginning of the race).

2 The first player throws the die and moves his or her marker along the game board path the number of spaces on the die.

3 The player then uses one of the vowel spellings in the flags alongside the game board to complete the word. The player states the word formed and spells it. If other players want to challenge the spelling, they can check the key card.

4 Each player continues in turn. The first player to reach FINISH (the checkered flag) wins.

Variations
• **Short Vowels:** Using self-stick tags, replace the incomplete words on the game board with incomplete words containing short vowels.

Replace the flags with short vowel spellings (*a, e, i, o, u, ea* as in *bread*).

Raceway
Game Board

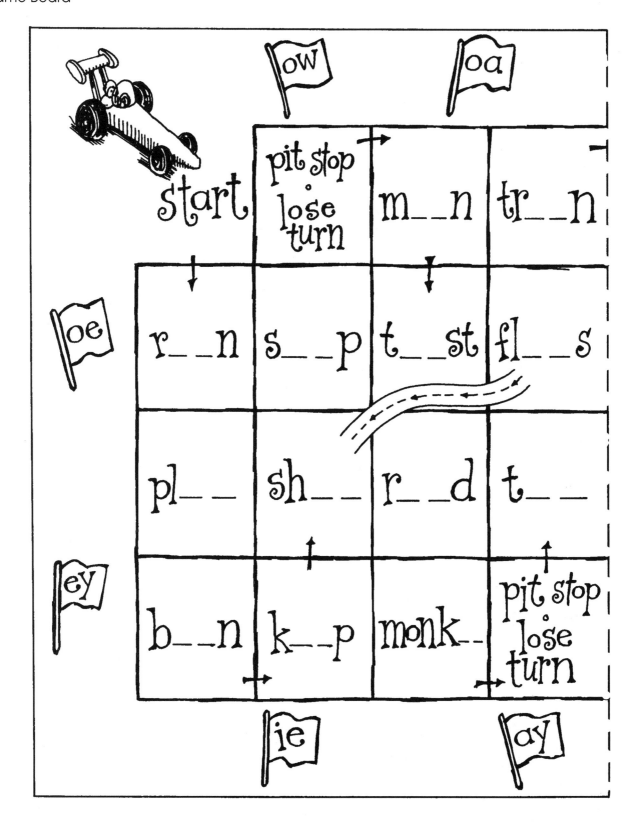

Raceway
Game Board

ee		ea		
hon__	g--s	s___	pit stop lose turn	w__t
__t	no gas! go back 2 spaces	gr___	cl__n	no gas! go back 2 spaces
d--p	k___	b__t	b__ch	l__f
fl__t	s--l	p---	tr___	finish

ai

Build-a-Word

Skill: consonant digraphs

MATERIALS

response sheet (see page 34)

game cards (see page 35)

pencils

timer

SETUP

▲ Distribute one game card and response sheet to each player or team.

TO PLAY

1 Using the letters and word parts on the word-building card, each player or team forms as many words as possible, recording words in the appropriate column on the response sheet. Each player or team has five minutes to form words. (Or whatever time you decide.) Use a timer or appoint a monitor to time the game.

2 After the allotted time, players or teams then switch game cards and the game resumes.

3 Players or teams receive one point for each word formed. The player or team with the most points at the end of the game wins.

Variations

• Make It More Challenging: Adjust the playing time. For example, limit playing time to three minutes.

• Make New Game Cards: Use different word parts or combinations of digraphs to make new game cards. Add the digraph *ph* to some of the cards.

• Play Cooperatively: Have students work together to form as many words as they can in five minutes.

Build-a-Word

Response Sheet

Name:	
ch	sh
th **3**	wh

Build-a-Word
Word-Building Cards

ch	sh
lun	ip
ri	ill
pin	ben
op	bru
ape	ine
fi	tra

th	wh
en	ink
ick	clo
ile	at
ing	iz
ba	ma
ich	ale

Blend TIC-TAC-TOE

Skill: consonant blends

MATERIALS

game boards (see pages 37–39)

pencils

SETUP

▲ Make copies of the game boards.

▲ Place the game boards in a folder. Have players select the game board they want. (You might want to laminate a set and have children use markers that wipe off. This way, players can reuse the games.)

TO PLAY

1 The game is similar to a standard game of tic-tac-toe. Each player must first choose to be either X's or O's.

2 In turn, each player then marks an X or an O on one square of the TIC-TAC-TOE grid. In order for a player to mark an X or an O on a square, he or she must first add one of the blends listed above the TIC-TAC-TOE grid to the word ending on the square to form a word. The player reads aloud the word. If both players agree that the word is correct, the player can mark that square.

3 The player who gets three X's or three O's in a row horizontally, vertically, or diagonally first wins.

Variations

• Add New Blends: Using the same game boards, replace the blends with digraphs and other 2- and 3-letter blends such as *ch*, *sh*, *th*, *wh*, *ph*, *gl*, *pr*, *sc*, *sl*, *sw*, *tw*, *spl*, *scr*, *spr*, *squ*, *str*, and *shr*.

• Add Endings: Reverse the game. Using a blank game board, write only the beginning blend or digraph. Students make words by adding ending phonograms.

Blend TIC-TAC-TOE
Game Board

bl	br	cl	cr	pl

_____ ack	_____ own	_____ ue
_____ ank	_____ ot	_____ ow
_____ ock	_____ ick	_____ ash

Blend TIC-TAC-TOE
Game Board

| fl | fr | dr | gr | tr |

____ y	____ ill	____ op
____ ew	____ ain	____ ip
____ ap	____ ash	____ ight

Blend TIC-TAC-TOE

Game Board

| sk | sm | sn | sp | st |

_____ oke	_____ ell	_____ all
_____ ack	_____ are	_____ eak
_____ iff	_____ unk	_____ ill

Match It!

Skill: consonant blends and digraphs

MATERIALS

game cards (see page 41)

SETUP

▲ Make multiple copies of the game cards.

▲ On each card write the word parts. For the word *black*, for example, write the letters *bl* to the far right of the game card and the letters *ack* to the far left of the card (see sample, left). In this way, students can read the words with greater ease as they form them. Use the following word list to begin: *bl/ack, tr/ee, ch/air, sh/op, st/amp, fl/at, sm/all, pl/ace, dr/aw.*

TO PLAY

1 Shuffle the cards and place the stack facedown. Give two cards to each player.

2 The first player draws a card from the stack. If the player can use the card to form a word with one other card in his or her hand, the player reads aloud the word and places the two cards down. If the player can't form a word, he or she keeps the cards. The next player takes a turn, proceeding in the same way.

3 When all the cards are gone from the stack, players draw cards from each other until all possible words can be formed. The player with the most cards at the end of the game wins.

Variations

• Make More Cards: Increase the card deck to 36 cards using the following words: *wh/ite, th/in, br/own, cl/ean, gr/een, sp/eak, spl/ash, pr/ice, gl/ow.* Make additional game cards using words that begin with other digraphs or blends. Divide the words between the blend or digraph and the phonogram.

• Spell It: Make game cards using your weekly spelling words.

Match it!

Game Cards

Roll, Pick, and Read

Skill: diphthongs

MATERIALS

game cards (see page 43)

die (see page 12)

paper and pencils

SETUP

▲ Make a copy of the game cards and the die. Using the die on page 12 as a pattern, make a die with the numbers 2 to 5 and the words *lose a turn.*

▲ Shuffle the game cards and spread them face-down on a table or place them in a bag.

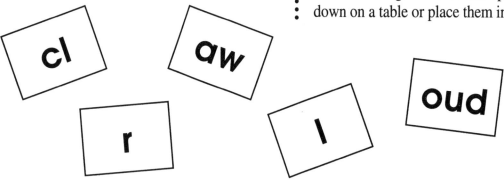

······· **TO PLAY** ·······

1 The first player rolls the die and selects the number of cards marked on the die. For example, if a player rolls a 5, he or she picks 5 cards from the bag or picks up 5 cards off the table.

2 Using the cards selected, the player tries to form as many words as possible, recording them on paper. Each word earns one point.

3 Each player continues in turn. The first player to earn 10 points wins.

Variations

• Vary the letters and word parts on the game cards by adding new sounds to the card deck. Most vowel patterns can be used.

• Silent Letters: Make new game cards with the words *lamb, comb, wrong, right, know, knee, climb, wrap, gnat.* Students pick the number of cards on the die, read the words, and identify the silent letters.

Roll, Pick, and Read
Game Cards

oud	ound	oil	oy
aul	ause	aw	oin
sp	m	awn	outh
h	c	p	l
cl	s	r	f
b	t	j	dr

Vowel Concentration

Skill: vowel digraph *oo*

MATERIALS

game cards (see page 45)

SETUP

▲ Make a copy of the game cards.

▲ Spread out the cards facedown on a table.

TO PLAY

1 In turn, each player turns over two cards and reads aloud the word on each card. If the two selected cards contain a rhyming pair, such as *book* and *look*, the player gets to keep the cards. If the cards do not rhyme, the player turns the cards over in their original position. The object of the game is to remember where words are located so that pairs can be formed in future turns.

2 Each player continues in turn until all the pairs have been found. The player with the most cards at the end of the game wins.

Variations

• Building Sentences: Players must use both rhyming words in sentences in order to earn the set.

• Add New Cards: Add new cards containing the following words: *shook, brook, wood, hood, bloom, broom, cool, pool, droop, hoop, goose, moose, pool, tool, stoop, scoop.*

• Diphthongs and Variant Vowels: Make cards using the following sets of words: *cow/now; flower/shower; mouth/south; cloud/loud; coin/join; soil/spoil; toy/boy; brown/clown; down/town; frown/gown; cause/pause; saw/claw; straw/draw; sound/round; mouse/house.*

Vowel Concentration

Game Cards

book	cook	
took	look	good
stood	moon	soon
spoon	noon	room
zoom	shoot	boot

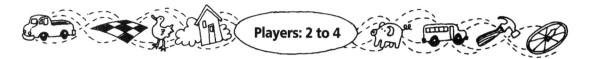

Back to the Barn

Skill: *r*-controlled vowels

MATERIALS

game board (see pages 47–48)

die (see page 12)

place marker for each player

SETUP

▲ Make a copy of the game board and die. Construct the die by folding along the dotted lines and using tape to attach the die tabs to the die squares.

TO PLAY

1 Each player chooses a place marker and puts it on START (the pasture gate).

2 The first player throws the die and moves his or her marker along the game board path the number of spaces on the die.

3 The player then reads the word on the game board space. If the player is unable to read the word, he or she loses a turn.

4 Each player continues in turn. The first player to reach FINISH (the barn) wins.

Variations
• Building Sentences: Players read the words they land on and use them in sentences.
• Vary the Game Board: Replace the words with other *r*-controlled words.
• Diphthongs and Variant Vowels: Using self-stick tabs, replace the *r*-controlled vowel words with words containing diphthongs and variant vowel spellings. You might wish to use the following word list: *boy, joy, toy, soil, coin, spoil, join, point, cause, pause, drawn, saw, claw, loud, cloud, round, sound, mouth, book, took, good, moon, room, boot, scoop.*

Back to the Barn
Game Board

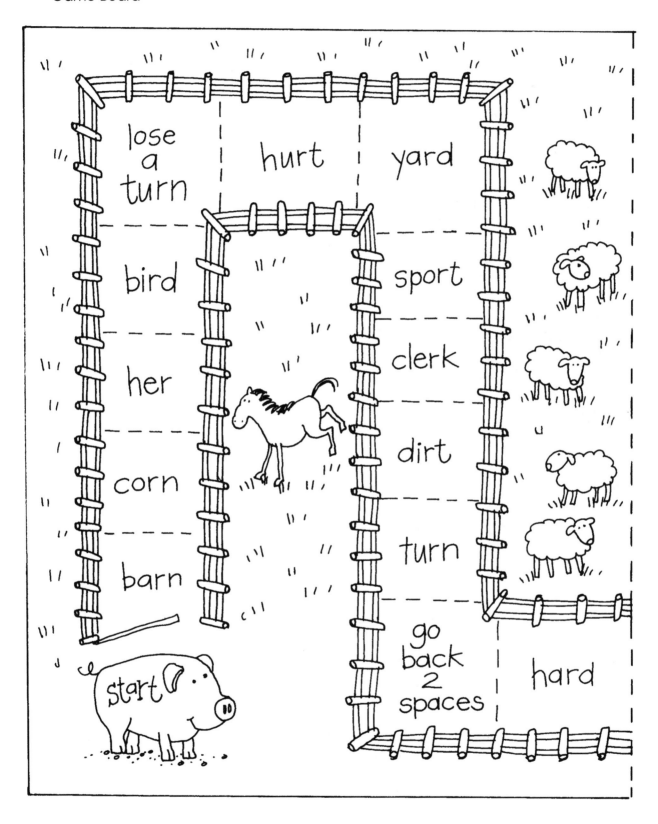

lose a turn

hurt

yard

bird

sport

clerk

her

dirt

corn

turn

barn

start

go back 2 spaces

hard

Back to the Barn

Game Board

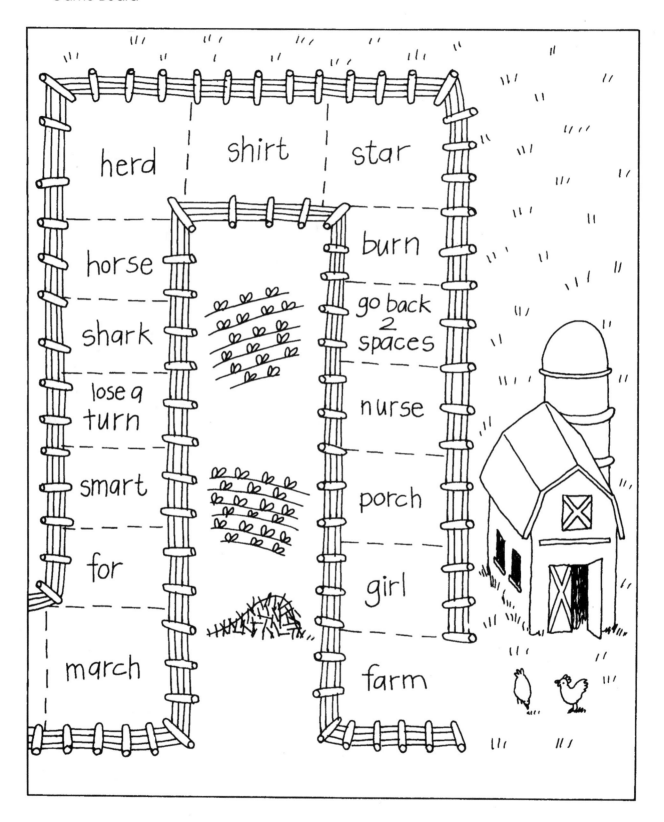

herd

shirt

star

horse

burn

shark

go back 2 spaces

lose a turn

nurse

smart

porch

for

girl

march

farm